Merrick Garland

Carolyn Kreshner

DEDICATION

This book is dedicated to my sister, Leanne and my father George L. Hubernly.

CONTENTS

ACKNOWLEDGMENTS

Thank you for the service to our country by so many great men (and women) throughout these last several years.

Merrick Brian Garland was born on November 13, 1952 in Chicago, Illinois. It is also in his land of birth that Garland was raised more specifically in the northern suburb of Chicago Lincolnwood. His mother, Shirley Garland, was a director of volunteer services for the Chicago Council for the Jewish Elderly. Cyril Garland, his father, was a businessman who ran Garland Advertising, a small business, from their home. Merrick was brought up in Conservative Judaism. His grandfather was a Jew who had found refuge in USA after fleeing anti-Semitism.

Garland has been married to his wife, Lynn, since 1987. Notably Lynn Garland's grandfather, Samuel Irving Rosenman, was a justice of the New York Supreme Court (a trial-level court) and a special counsel to Presidents Franklin D. Roosevelt and Harry S. Truman. Garland and his wife have two daughters, Rebecca and Jessica; both are graduates of Yale University.

Garland is a resident of Bethesda, Maryland

CHAPTER 2
EDUCATION AND LEGAL TRAINING

Merrick attended Niles West High School, Illinois. His diligence saw him become a Presidential Scholar as well as the National Merit Scholar. He graduated as a class valedictorian and earned a scholarship to Harvard College.

In 1974, he graduated as a valedictorian with *Phi Beta Kappa* in Social Studies as well as an *Bachelor of Arts summa cum laude* from Harvard College, He proceeded to Harvard Law School where he graduated Juries Doctor *magna cum laude* in 1977.

The federal judge is the chief judge of the United States Courts of Appeal for the District of Columbia Circuit where he has serve since 1997.

After graduating, he served as a law clerk Judge Henry J. Friendly of the U.S. Court of Appeals for the Second Circuit a period spanning from 1977 to 1978. He also served Justice William J. Brennan, Jr. of the Supreme Court of the United States as a law clerk from 1978 to 1979. Garland then became a special assistance to Attorney General Benjamin Civiletti from 1979 from 1981. He then shifted to private sector by joining Arnold and Porter law firm where he became a partner from 1985 to 1989. While at Arnold and Porter, his area of specialty was corporate litigation. While still working in the firm, he was also a lecturer in Harvard Law School. He also published his articles in Harvard Law Review as well as Yale Law Journal. The articles were about antitrust laws, the area which he was teaching at Harvard.

Garland returned to public sector as an assistant US Attorney in the US Attorney's office in the District of Columbia in 1989. As a prosecutor, his capacity saw representation of the government in criminal cases. In 1992, Garland went back to Arnold and Porter where he served until 1993. Upon institution of Clinton's government, he rejoined public service in 1993 as a deputy assistant attorney general in the US Department of Justice, Criminal Division. His boss, Deputy Attorney General Jamie Gorelick, asked him to be his deputy the following year.

It is in this capacity that Garland played a leading role in the investigation and prosecution of the Oklahoma City bombers and other domestic-terrorism cases, one of the responsibilities under the docket. Other cases supervised by Garland during his tenure included the Atlanta Olympics bombing investigations as well as UNABOM prosecution. During the Oklahoma City bombers investigation, Garland insisted on going to Oklahoma City in the aftermath of the attack to examine the crime scene as well as oversee the investigation in readiness for the prosecution.

Further, he represented the government at the preliminary hearings of Timothy McVeigh and Terry Nichols. The two were the main defendants in the Oklahoma case. Despite offering to lead the trial team, Garland could not be present because he was needed at the Justice Department headquarters. However, he helped pick the team and supervised it from Washington. The trial involved major decisions, including the choice to seek the death penalty for McVeigh and Nichols. At the end of the process, Garland won praise for his outstanding work on the case from the Republican governor of Oklahoma, Frank Keating.

CHAPTER 3
APPOINTMENT TO THE D.C. CIRCUIT

On September 6, 1995, Garland was nominated by President Bill Clinton to the U.S. Court of Appeals D.C. Circuit seat vacated by Abner J. Mikva. Further, he received a "unanimously well-qualified" committee rating from the American Bar Association (ABA) Standing Committee on the Federal Judiciary. This is its highest rating.

On December 1, 1995, Garland received a hearing before the U.S. Senate Judiciary Committee. Senate Republicans would not schedule a vote on Garland's confirmation simply over a dispute on whether to fill his predecessor's seat and in particular having an eleventh seat. The dispute was not about concerns over Garland's qualifications. After a delay in Senate confirmation, Garland took the bench in 1997.

After winning the November 1996 presidential election, Clinton re-nominated Garland on January 7, 1997. His confirmation vote was brought to Senate floor on March 19, 1997. By a 76-23 vote, he was confirmed. On the next day, Garland received his judicial commission. Including senators Mitch McConnell, Chuck Grassley and Jeff Sessions, all of the 23 votes against Garland came from Republicans. The opposition was centered on the question for the need of an eleventh seat on the D.C. Circuit. However, most of the Republican senators voted to confirm Garland. They included Senators John

McCain, Orrin Hatch, Susan Collins, and Jim Inhofe. were among those who voted against Garland.

CHAPTER 4
SERVICE ON THE D.C. CIRCUIT, REPUTATION, AND JUDICIAL PHILOSOPHY

There are various opinion statements that have been given by members of the public including influential persons.

Described by Nina Totenberg and Carrie Johnson of NPR as "a moderate liberal, with a definite pro-prosecution bent in criminal cases" Garland is considered a judicial moderate and a centrist.

Tom Goldstein, the publisher of SCOTUSblog, wrote in 2010 that "Judge Garland's record demonstrates that he is essentially the model, neutral judge. He is acknowledged by all to be brilliant. His opinions avoid unnecessary, sweeping pronouncements." Garland has "tended to take a broader view" of First Amendment rights. In a number of split decisions on environmental law in the D.C. Circuit Court, Garland has "favored contested EPA regulations and actions when challenged by industry, and in other cases he has accepted challenges brought by environmental groups". In cases involving the Freedom of Information Act and similar provisions related to government transparency, "Judge Garland's rulings reflect a preference for open government."

Judge Garland dissented from the denial of a rehearing in the case of Whitman vs. American Trucking Ass'ns, Inc. (2001). The decision D.C. Circuit by was later to be reversed by the Supreme Court, in an opinion by Justice Scalia. Other cases that depicted Garland's view included al Odah v. United States (2003). Through his panel, it was unanimously held that challenges from prisoners in the Guantanamo Bay detention camp could not be heard by federal courts. However, in Rasul v. Bush (2004) the decision was reversed by the Supreme Court, over a dissent by Justice Scalia.

He expressed his utmost admirations to the work of Justice Brennan, whom he had clerked, as well as Chief Justice John Marshall. This was during the Senate confirmation hearings held in December 1995 to consider Garland's nomination to the D.C. Circuit. He also adored the writing style of Justice

Oliver Wendell Holmes.

He became chief judge on February 12, 2013.

CHAPTER 5
SUPREME COURT NOMINATION

Before ultimately receiving a nomination in 2016, Garland had been considered twice for the Supreme Court (in 2009 and in 2010). In 2009, following the announcement by Justice David Souter that he would retire, Garland was considered as one of nine finalists for the post, which ultimately went to Sonia Sotomayor, then a judge of the Second Circuit. After the April 2010 announcement by Justice John Paul Stevens that he would retire, Garland was again widely seen as a leading contender for a nomination to the Supreme Court of the United States. President Barack Obama interviewed

Garland, among others,for the vacancy. In May, Senator Orrin G. Hatch, Republican of Utah, said he would help Obama if Garland was nominated, calling Garland "a consensus nominee" and predicting that Garland would win Senate confirmation with bipartisan support. Obama nominated Solicitor General of the United States Elena Kagan, who was confirmed in August 2010.

On February 13, 2016, Justice Antonin Scalia died. The next day, Senate Republicans led by Majority Leader Mitch McConnell issued a statement that they would not consider any nominee put forth by Obama, saying that a Supreme Court nomination should be left to the next President. Scholars and experts noted that such a refusal to consider a presidential Supreme Court nominee is unprecedented. On March 4, The New York Times reported that Garland was being vetted by the Obama administration as a potential nominee. A week later, Garland was named as one of three judges on the President's "short list" (along with Judge Sri Srinivasan, also of the D.C. Circuit, and Judge Paul J. Watford of the Ninth Circuit). Obama interviewed all three leading contenders, as well as two others who were considered: Judge Jane L. Kelly of the Eighth Circuitand Judge Ketanji Brown Jackson of the U.S. District Court for the District of Columbia. On March 16, Obama formally nominated Garland. Garland has more federal judicial experience than any Supreme Court nominee in history.

CHAPTER 6
MEMBERSHIPS AND COMMITTEE SERVICE

Garland served as co-chair of the administrative law section of the District of Columbia Bar from 1991 to 1994.

Garland is a member of the American Law Institute.

In 2003, Garland was elected to the Harvard Board of Overseers, completing the unexpired term of Deval Patrick, who had stepped down from the board. Garland served as president of the overseers for 2009–2010.

ABOUT THE AUTHOR

Carolyn Kreshner is an author, philanthropist, and lover of birds.

CPSIA information can be obtained
at www.ICGtesting.com
Printed in the USA
LVHW101447170519
618241LV00025B/685/P

9 781530 603190